Work As Worship

Mack Arrington, PCC

How do you practice your faith in Christ at work?

Bailey Blue Heron Publishers
3808 Rappahannock Ct
Greensboro, NC 27407

Phone: 336.856.1600 · www.mackarrington.com

ISBN: 978-0-9911791-0-7

Library of Congress Control Number (LCCN): 2013921149

Work As Worship

Contents	**Page**

Knowing Whose You Are

I have been an executive and life coach since 2001. I have coached people in times of joy and difficulty to deal with life and to define success in their own terms. When my clients have included their faith in Christ Jesus as their foundation for coaching, they had an immediate reference point for their lives that I fully engaged and that I coached them to deepen.

Many, many of us face the difficulty of letting work get in the way of our growth in our Lord. We know that Christ is our Standard, but we have difficulty verbalizing the Standards of Christ and practicing them at work. When we are not clear on our standards, it is more difficult to set our boundaries. When our standards are not respected and our boundaries are not maintained, we are out of integrity with ourselves and with our faith.

Our standards and boundaries are intimately connected, but what are they? How do we clarify, maintain and live them in our work? What gets in our way, and how do we set our boundaries according to what Father God wants—more than what we want for ourselves?

Sometimes a book will help. Sometimes you need someone like a coach to come along side you and offer assistance. Always you need Christ as your Savior and the Holy Spirit as your Teacher. Know that you are bought with a high price, and in Christ you belong to Him. Remember whose you are.

Mack Arrington, PCC

Work As Worship: How's This Working for You?

Kay and Warren are Christian believers who worked together doing the same work in the same department for the same company. One day, the Human Resources Director called Kay into her office for a conference. Kay was told that as of the beginning of next week, she would be promoted to supervisor in her department. Kay was also told that Warren would be laid off at the same time, and that she would have to deliver this news to Warren on her first day as supervisor. The director told Kay to finish the day in her old position, but tomorrow she was to report to the Human Resources Department to take care of some paperwork and to enter a supervisor training program for the rest of the week.

As she left the director's office, her thoughts turned to Warren. He had a family and medical bills to pay. He was working to put his kids through school. How could she spend the rest of the day working next to him, knowing that next week she would have to let him go? What could she tell him when he asked her about the meeting with their director? How would this work out?

Situations like this can be difficult, especially if you are a Christian and want to do the right thing. On the one hand, Kay is loyal to her coworker and fellow believer Warren. On the other hand, she has responsibilities to her own job and family. What about the third hand—the hand of God that she wants to find in this hour of needing help?

You could say that I coach people to play and win their game of life. I keep finding Christian believers whose lives get messy because they have never fully clarified their own standards and boundaries. They want to please and honor our Father by the way they live, but they keep ambushing themselves along the way. They often set themselves up for their own ambush without realizing it.

Life can come at you pretty fast and hard, full of surprises and challenges to our faith.

Have you ever been caught off-guard or taken by surprise by some event or by how someone acted or what they said?

Even more, have you ever wished you had said or done something differently? Have you ever rehearsed just the right thing to say or do, only to have it turn out wrong? This can have a terrible impact in the workplace as well as the home.

What will you do when someone at work disrespects you or your faith? How do you plan to respond when certain music, video or other entertainment dishonors your faith? Who will you seek when you need a prayer partner or wise counsel? How will you teach people to respect your boundaries? What will you do when you are surrounded by a great cloud of witnesses?

> **Hebrews 12:1 Therefore, since we are surrounded by so great a cloud of witnesses, let us also lay aside every weight, and sin which clings so closely, and let us run with endurance the race that is set before us**

Our Bible says that we all run the race. This book can be a tool for staying faithful in the race. It gives you a place to anticipate the challenges you will face and a way to correct and further to develop your responses. Yes, I understand that Father controls the outcomes and we don't. Yet, in our context as believers, we need to pay attention to what Father wants us to do to stand for Him in a fallen world. How will you be faithful in finishing the race?

We will consider:

We are created to worship our Creator.

How do we worship our Creator?

How might we worship our Creator at work?

How do we make our work environment a place of worship?

How come the focus on *Work As Worship*?

I find one challenge in our faith is that it is not human nature to carry a sense of worship throughout the day. When we go to work, to our jobs, our businesses and our duties, we have all kinds of reasons and distractions that can take us away from being centered in Christ. This is not what Father wants. But what does He want and do we want it too? As you will see, **worship is the main activity that connects us to all the resources Father provides for us**.

I believe the joy of the Lord is our strength (Ne 8:10). We miss a lot of joy because we don't take time to know our Lord. When we lose joy, we lose heart, we lose strength and then we just lose, period. Not a good strategy.

In this book you will find recommendations on how to develop worship as a practice at your work. Just as a team develops and practices a strategy and actions for winning the race, you have the opportunity to create your own strategy and actions for winning the race that is set before you in Christ. You will get to consider, develop and practice what works for you, and hopefully share some of your practice with others. Our overall strategy is to develop an ongoing sense of worship by creating space in our day for worship, and to develop this as an ongoing practice. The challenge will be for you to decide and practice the actions that will support your particular race.

One other thing. At the end of each chapter you will find questions under the heading ***Considerations for your playbook,*** and at the end of this book you will find a page titled ***The Plan—Your Work As Worship Program***. Most of us have become highly trained and practiced at doing *work as non-worship*. It will be important for your success to plan your plan. You might want to start a journal or notebook to capture your thoughts and the insights you that will gain from drawing near to our Father at work, and to develop how you will shift into *work-as-worship* to our Most High God. Whether you call it a *playbook, planbook* or *guidebook*, just as we have trained ourselves to do work as work, we have to re-train ourselves by repeatedly running the play, practicing the plan, and following the guide to train ourselves for work as worship.

A powerful prayer prayed for you

First thing, I want you to know that the most powerful prayer has been prayed for you by Christ Jesus Himself. He prays that we will be one in Him, just as He is one with Father. This is the Lord's prayer that was actually prayed by the Lord. It's the beginning play in our playbook.

Prayer excerpts from John 17:

> 6 "I have revealed you to those whom you gave me out of the world.
>
> 20 "I pray also for those who will believe in me through their message, 21 that all of them may be one, Father, just as you are in me and I am in you. May they also be in us so that the world may believe that you have sent me. 22 I

> have given them the glory that you gave me, that they may be one as we are one — 23 I in them and you in me—so that they may be brought to complete unity. Then the world will know that you sent me and have loved them even as you have loved me.
>
> 24 "Father, I want those you have given me to be with me where I am, and to see my glory, the glory you have given me because you loved me before the creation of the world.
> 25 "Righteous Father, though the world does not know you, I know you, and they know that you have sent me. 26 I have made you known to them, and will continue to make you known in order that the love you have for me may be in them and that I myself may be in them."

Complete unity is the main goal. Worship is how we get there. But how do we worship at work? Before we can answer that question, let's consider a bigger one...What does Father God want for Himself?

As human beings, it can be easy to focus on what we want from God—blessings, health, wealth, love, children, adventure, the next sale to keep our businesses going and the next promotion to keep our careers on track. We know that Father God wants good things for us, and that there are things He wants us to do. But just what does Father God want for Himself?

I will answer this question shortly. First I must write something that has to be obvious to believers: **We have to get to know Father for Who He Is, and not who we want Him to be**. We are created in His Image: He is not created in ours. We are created for His purpose: He is not created for our convenience. Therefore, I believe it very important to pay attention and to learn what Father wants.

In this book, I am asking you do three things you might not have done before.

First, view your work as a way to know Father more deeply.

Second, do or start doing your work as one form of worship.

Third, think of how you can find and share the joy of the Lord at work.

Your work as a way to know Father more deeply

Father **worked** in creating our world, and then He rested:

> **Genesis 2:2 By the seventh day God had finished the work he had been doing; so on the seventh day he rested from all his work. 3 Then God blessed the seventh day and made it holy, because on it he rested from all the work of creating that he had done.**

I often say that one way to really get to know someone is to work with them or play with them. Be it a job, a business, a mission, a calling, a service or something else, our work is a way to get to know Father. Father worked to create the world. We work to fulfill Father's pleasure and purpose. When we do work, we are doing something that Father did. When we willingly and intentionally bring Father into our work, He will teach the value of doing work in His way. We will learn to pay attention to what God is doing in our work.

Do your work as one form of worship

When we think of all the hours we spend working, two questions arise:

Is work something that you do to pay your bills, meet some needs, have nice things, maintain your freedom and financially support your faith, calling or missions?

—or—

Is work something you do with Father God as a way to learn His ways, draw closer to Him, discern His will for your life and fulfill His purpose?

If you engage with your work as worship, your work days can become a time for our Father to communicate His presence to you, and for you to develop an ongoing sense of His presence. Stop now for a few moments and answer this question:

Do you want an ongoing sense of God's presence throughout your days at work?
❑ Yes ❑ No ❑ Maybe?

It can be so easy to focus on work as, well, as work. It can be a new idea and experience to engage work as worship. Considering how much effort and focus we invest in doing our jobs, it can take some effort on our part to train ourselves to experience Father at work and experience work as worship.

Think of how you can find and share the joy of the Lord at work

I want for you to find His joy and His strength. You get this by knowing Him yourself. You can begin by thinking about how to turn work into worship. Consider how you can work so that you invite the Father to break into your busy day.

Helpful Tips Along the Way

- If you write something down, you are 37% more likely to do it. What might you want to write at the end of each section to keep on track?
- 10 minutes per work day for 20 workdays per month is 40 hours a year. For every 10 minutes of worship you can add to a work day, you add a whole week per year to worship Father.

- The average person spends 20 minutes a day looking for their keys. If you remember to keep your keys always in the same place, you can get an extra couple of weeks of worship each year!
- The average CEO spends 40 minutes a day looking for a piece of paper he had a while ago. How many weeks is this?
- Every minute you spend planning saves between 4–12 minutes of implementation. 15 minutes saves 1–3 hours. What might Father do with your extra time?
- Remember that you have requirements and you have choices. Look for your choices.

God Has A Vision for What He Wants

We human beings often have a vision or a dream of the life we want to create. We believe that if we attain that vision or dream, our life becomes a dream come true.

The question we face is: **What is God's vision?**

When we look to the Bible, we find God's vision. Not surprisingly, His vision involves us.

> Jeremiah 24:7 I will give them a heart to know me, that I am the Lord. **They will be my people, and I will be their God**, for they will return to me with all their heart.
>
> Jeremiah 31:33 For this is the covenant that I will make with the house of Israel after those days, declares the Lord: I will put my law within them, and I will write it on their hearts. And **I will be their God, and they shall be my people**.
>
> Jeremiah 32:38 **And they shall be my people, and I will be their God.**
>
> Ezekiel 11:20 that they may walk in my statutes and keep my rules and obey them. **And they shall be my people, and I will be their God.**
>
> Ezekiel 14:11 that the house of Israel may no more go astray from me, nor defile themselves anymore with all their transgressions, but **that they may be my people and I**

may be their God, declares the Lord God."

Ezekiel 37:23 They shall not defile themselves anymore with their idols and their detestable things, or with any of their transgressions. But I will save them from all the backslidings in which they have sinned, and will cleanse them; and **they shall be my people, and I will be their God**.

Ezekiel 37:27 My dwelling place shall be with them, and **I will be their God, and they shall be my people**.

Zechariah 8:8 and I will bring them to dwell in the midst of Jerusalem. And **they shall be my people, and I will be their God**, in faithfulness and in righteousness."

Revelation 21:3 And I heard a loud voice from the throne saying, "Behold, the dwelling place of God is with man. He will dwell with them, and **they will be his people, and God himself will be with them as their God**.

Do you get the sense that Father wants to be deeply acknowledged as God by a people who are blessed as they follow and fellowship in His presence?

What must we do to be God's people, and to make God be our God?

God's vision centers around worshipping Him as the Creator and Savior of the World, and **I believe it centers around a very specific form of worship**. It is not the kind of worship that prays for God's blessing upon us, to meet our needs or to heal our lives. It is not the kind of worship in meditating upon the scriptures and the various attributes of God. It is not the kind of worship that engages fasting and physical disciplines.

Yes, these and other disciplines are often practiced as forms of worship, but I mean the worship of God purely as our loving Father. To bless the name of our Lord, to praise Him for His goodness, to recount how He has blessed us, to feel a deep sense of thankfulness and appreciation, to enter into a sense of His presence for the simple purpose of being wrapped in His presence and held by His love. It is the kind of worship that begins in the privacy and intimacy of your prayer closet when you are alone and seeking to touch the throne of Father. It is this kind of worship shared corporately with others of like mind. This is the worship that sustains us when times are difficult. It is the kind of worship that is so hard to find and practice because so many things distract or detain us. I offer this quote:

> **"It is in the process of being worshipped that God communicates His presence to men."**
> **—C. S. Lewis**

If we are to make God to be our God and if we are to be His people, then we want and need to participate in making God's vision come true.

Considerations for your playbook:

When do you make time in your day to have time alone to worship? If you don't already make time, how and when will you start?

What will you do to worship Father?

Bless His Name, praise, recount His great deeds throughout history, recount His blessings in your own life, be quiet and sense His presence, and/or something else?

How do we participate in making God's vision come true?

In particular, how might we do this in our work?

Why We Are Here

As Christians, we are created to worship the Creator and be in His presence, this is part of who we are. Many of us have been taught that the workplace is no place for practicing or talking about our faith. Sharing our faith can cause conflict. But with some understanding, it can be done quite effectively. Allow me to share a personal story to illustrate.

> I came to work one day and was told that a supervisor in our small company had just been taken to the hospital emergency room. I strongly felt that we needed to pray for this supervisor, but I had no idea how this would be taken because this was simply not done in the work environment. In response to my urging from the Holy Spirit, I said to several of my colleagues that I felt we needed to gather and pray for the supervisor. As we gathered in an office down the hall, I was very surprised at who attended and joined into the prayers. Upon returning to work, the supervisor also expressed thanks for our "prayer meeting." It was as though the Lord used the emergency as a way to bring us together and open new relationships for those who were of the same mind and same faith.

I learned that Father has drawn many to Himself who do not wear the cross or the fish or the dove symbols for all to see. We are here to glorify Father and love Him with all our heart, soul, mind and strength, and to love each other, but it can be difficult to know who will pray and who will help unless we can share our faith in word and deed. I also learned that when something is going wrong, even the nonbelievers will seek out those who will pray if they can find us.

We spend many hours working, preparing for working, and commuting to and from work each week. Are we missing opportunities during these times to invite the presence of our Lord in worship?

> **Isaiah 55:6 Seek the Lord while he may be found; call upon him while he is near;**

As I write this line, why not practice the Presence of Christ Jesus being here looking over my shoulder? If we teach ourselves to practice a sense of Godly presence, what impact will this have on our days? Is He present with us when we do our jobs, play our games and take out the trash? How will we do these things differently when we practice His presence in the moment?

As you read this line,
why not practice the Presence
as though Christ Jesus is looking
over your shoulder?
—Take a couple of deep breaths,
practice His Presence.

***

What are some things that can distract us or keep us from worship at work?

In the beginning, Adam had a wonderful and meaningful job description. He had to name the animals, care for the garden, fellowship with Father and not eat from a certain tree. Some of the wonderful things about having work to do is that we can find meaning in the job (ok, sometimes you might have to look hard). It can be a way to be part of a community, a way to contribute, to support ourselves, to have a sense of pride in doing a job well done, and to provide for our families and others in need. We can also have such a focus on these great things that we forget to include fellowship with Father throughout our days.

The principle I want you to get here is simple: You tend to get good at whatever you practice. If you practice doing your job well, you tend to get better at doing your job. If you practice leaving Father out of your day, you can get very good at this too. If practice makes perfect, we don't want to become perfect at leaving God out of our days at work.

The Attitude of Worship.

Part of the challenge of including worship in our work day is that we can only focus on one thing at a time. There may be several things going on around us at the same time, and we can sometimes switch between them quickly and easily. However, we tend to have only one focus at a time. Does this mean that we must choose between paying attention to our work versus paying attention to our Lord?

> **Colossians 3:23 Whatever you do, work heartily, as for the Lord and not for men,**

I believe the answer is to be found in the attitude of how we approach our work.

Are you working for a paycheck, or are you working for the Lord?

Are you just putting in your time until the weekend, or are

you putting in time to His glory?

Are you busy hating your job, or are you busy enjoying fellowship with the Holy Spirit throughout your day while you are at your job?

Do you feel your talents are wasted on this job, or are your talents available for wherever the Lord has you today?

Are you working to build a product, or are you working to build the Kingdom of God?

Is your work your mission, or does it support your mission, or is it just a job?

Are you working to offer a service, or are you serving the Living God of eternity?

Though most of us cannot think of Father continuously, we can teach and practice a continuous ***attitude of faith*** that honors Him in all that we do.

Let's take a look at some of the things that get in the way of work as worship.

Busy-ness, the easy justification.

It can be very easy to fill our days with busy-ness. We have calls to make and answer, messages that take so much of our time. I recall some old research showing that most interruptions are less important than the work they interrupt. How can we be too busy to pay attention to the Ancient of Days and our Creator?

You might respond, "Are you asking me to add worship to my daily do list? My day already runs out before I can even get my work done?"

Actually, I am not asking you to add worship to an already overcrowded day. I'm asking you to make worship a context for your overcrowded day. It can be so easy to get busy with the task at hand. When our list of "things to do" keeps growing, our sense of His Presence can become just another checkbox on the list instead of being the context that supports our work throughout the day.

Even on the days when your schedule sets itself and you stay busy—for the whole ten hours you are at work, you can choose to work in an attitude of worship.

Yes, Father gives us a choice.

I coach people on *The Myth of Time Management*. You cannot manage time, you cannot yet travel one second back to the past nor one moment faster to the future. Time is not manageable, but *our choices* are. Here is one choice: choose to include Father throughout our day and practice this until it becomes ingrained as a habit, or choose to suffer through.

At Koinonia Farm near Americus, Georgia, they ring a bell three times a day so that everyone can choose to stop and worship. Note that I said everyone can **choose** to stop and worship. In visiting there, it was wonderful to have moments of fellowship throughout the day and to share a sense of Father's presence. If you don't have a bell that rings, can you identify another reminder to break you out of your busy-ness and into Father's presence?

Fear of what you have to lose.

Sharing your faith at work can be risky as well as rewarding. I learned this firsthand.

> When I first received Christ I was excited to share the joy I had experienced and thought to be respectful and God-honoring in how I shared my faith. My manager called me into his office to discuss my beliefs, but it turned out to be a one-sided conversation. In short he said that some of my fellow employees had complained and he asked that I keep my faith to myself. Not meaning to offend, I became more

careful about asking permission before sharing my faith.

If you take some time to get to know your co-workers, then they can get a sense of what kind of person you are by the example of your life. Many will be open to this kind of sharing because it is part of who you are. Instead of launching full bore into this kind of conversation, asking permission can be very important. Asking permission can be as simple as saying, "I want to respect your beliefs; would you be ok with me sharing something with you about my faith in Christ? You can say, 'No,' and that would be ok too."

We have to be sensitive to those around us who don't know the Lord, who don't know the Christian faith, and who have been hurt by well-meaning Christians along the way.

> **1Corinthians 9:22 To the weak I became weak, that I might win the weak. I have become all things to all people, that by all means I might save some. 23 I do it all for the sake of the gospel, that I may share with them in its blessings.**

Often the better way is to come alongside your co-workers and be helpful in getting to know each other. Let them see your good work and the joy in the Lord which is our strength, and be ready to share this when the opportunity arises to share.

I also admit that sometimes our fears are well-founded. Sometimes sharing our faith can cost us friendships, partners, jobs and more. After my manager told me to keep quiet about my faith, I soon left for another employer.

Guilt and Shame

Have you ever let guilt and shame stop you from sharing your faith? Have you ever let guilt and shame stop you from fully participating in church or other activities? The Bible shows that our Father does not mean for guilt or shame to stand in the way of His ministry or mission for us. Our Father desires that we approach the throne of grace with confidence.

> **Hebrews 4:16 Let us then with confidence draw near to the throne of grace, that we may receive mercy and find grace to help in time of need.**

This is the reason Christ Jesus came, died and rose from the grave. He did it to give us direct access to the throne of heaven, to be God's people and have God be our God. He did it so we could receive forgiveness and so that guilt and shame could not be used as weapons to beat us and keep us from doing His will.

We start with worship alone in our prayer closets to seek Father, for Him to communicate and reveal His presence to us. We confirm that His presence and His leading is in agreement with His Word in the Bible. We seek to be clear on what He wants us to do, and we confess our shortcomings and pray for His grace so that, ideally, nothing gets in the way of doing His will in our lives.

> **1John 1:9 If we confess our sins, he is faithful and just to forgive us our sins and to cleanse us from all unrighteousness.**

Disarming our spiritual enemy is just a confession away.

You see
He sets us free
Free with Him to be

Filled with His grace
We will see Him face to face
When we finish running in His race

Not only has Father called us to be His people, but also has given us Christ Jesus as the means to lay aside every weight that can possibly get in the way of worshipping Him in Spirit and in truth and accomplishing His will in our lives on earth.

> **1John 3:18 My little children, let us not love in word, neither in tongue; but in deed and in truth. 19 And hereby we know that we are of the truth, and shall assure our hearts before him. 20 For if our heart condemn us, God is greater than our heart, and knoweth all things. 2 Beloved, if our heart condemn us not, then have we confidence toward God.**

You might feel a sense of guilt and shame, but know that Father does not intend for your guilt and shame to keep you from your purpose nor separate you from His love and care for you. Father is bigger than your guilt and shame and is ready to forgive. Do not let guilt and shame become like a bat that us used to beat you down. To disarm your inner and outer critics, confess your shortcomings and keep moving in Father's will for your life.

Fear of Making a Mistake

Fear can cause us to freeze in our tracks.

> **2Timothy 1:7 For God gave us a spirit not of fear but of power and love and self-control.**

I once heard a sermon in which the preacher preached, "The only thing God cannot redeem is nothing." This can be a fun statement to debate, but the point here is that the folks who don't make mistakes are the folks who don't do anything. True, some of us give Him more to redeem than others, but God is able to redeem and to use our mistakes for His glory.

I have found it is never wrong to offer the love of God to anyone. Though there have been times when this offer has been ill-received, I have been amazed at how offering His love has been received with thanks, and how offering His love in a sincere and humble manner has brought many touchy situations to a peaceable end.

> My wife and I went out to lunch with a missionary couple who had come to visit our church. We were very surprised when the missionaries asked the waiter if they could pray for him. We were even more surprised when the waiter shared his deep concern for his elderly parents and asked us to pray for specific things concerning his parents.

Since that time, I have found a receptive response whenever I ask how to pray for someone. Just in case I overstep and cause offense, I am ready to say, "Please excuse me" and ask for forgiveness.

As the Bible says, God has given us a spirit of power, love and a sound mind; let us reach out to others in His name, and reach out to Father in our worship for His guidance in becoming His people.

Criticism and Hypocrisy

The question comes to mind, "Who are you to criticize me when you are not doing so well yourself?" The cliche answer comes back, "Christians are not perfect, just forgiven." It can be absolutely mind-boggling to find someone who feels like you criticize their non-Christian lifestyle when you have not yet said anything to them about it. Sometimes your very presence can convict people of their ungodliness.

Face it, people who work with you will see when you have a bad hair day. They see you when you make mistakes, lose your temper and when your attitude or behavior is not Godly. God will forgive you, but some of your associates will not. They will view your efforts of worship as you being "holier than thou" or being a hypocrite. If you do not use this as a bat for beating on yourself, they will be glad to do it for you.

My answer to this is pretty simple: *fail with gusto and admit it.* When you confess your failure and your hypocrisy, Father will forgive and can continue to work through the person that you are. Your confession tends to disarm your opponents too. "Yes, I did get angry at the supply guy for leaving my order back at the warehouse. I apologized to him for what I said and made it right. I asked him to forgive me and he said he did." We cannot help but make mistakes, we can help how we fix them.

Considerations for Your Playbook:

What gets in the way of your worshipping?

What gets in the way of your worshipping at work?

How might you get out of your way?

God Is Present in the Present

The Lord is always present with us. We fellowship with God in the present, He communicates his presence in the present. How do we find God in the present?

> **Jeremiah 29:13 You will seek me and find me, when you seek me with all your heart.**

As human beings, when we meet someone special to us, we want to spend time together. Sometimes we want to spend time just with that special someone and share things important to our hearts, our longings, our troubles. You don't usually share these kinds of things with a stranger. You don't get to know a stranger very well if you do all the talking.

Father is the same way. He desires to share close and intimate things with us. We know his vision: to be our God and for us to be His people, but it's like we keep embracing and yet resisting what we need to do to be His people. In the Old Testament, the people had the opportunity to have God to lead them directly, and do you know they said?

> **1Samuel 8:4 Then all the elders of Israel gathered together and came to Samuel at Ramah and said to him, "Behold, you are old and your sons do not walk in your**

ways. Now appoint for us a king to judge us like all the nations."

7 And the Lord said to Samuel, "Obey the voice of the people in all that they say to you, for they have not rejected you, but they have rejected me from being king over them.

Our Father wanted to lead His people Himself, but what did His people say? They said they wanted a king like all the other kingdoms. They said they wanted someone to stand between them and Father, so Father gave them King Saul. Did they miss an opportunity to truly know Father or what?

We serve our Father who wants to know us and to be known intimately. He wants to make His presence known to us, and once we embrace this in our hearts, how do we learn to know Him? Here is what happened with the prophet Elijah:

1Kings 19:11 And he said, "Go out and stand on the mount before the Lord." And behold, the Lord passed by, and a great and strong wind tore the mountains and broke in pieces the rocks before the Lord, but the Lord was not in the wind. And after the wind an earthquake, but the Lord was not in the earthquake. 12 And after the earthquake a fire, but the Lord was not in the fire. And after the fire the sound of a low whisper. 13 And when Elijah heard it, he wrapped his face in his cloak and went out and stood at the entrance of the cave.

Father often speaks as a low whisper, or as some translations have it, a still, small voice—a voice that we might not hear unless we have spent time to get to know the sound of His voice. His voice will always be in agreement with His Word in the Bible—but what if you find contradictions and discrepancies in the Bible? I have come to believe that when we perceive contradictions and discrepancies, this is Father's invitation to go deeper into relationship with Him until we find that place where contradictions and discrepancies give way into understanding and unity.

What does Father have to say about how we think compared to how He thinks?

> **Isaiah 55:8 For my thoughts are not your thoughts, neither are your ways my ways, declares the Lord. 9 For as the heavens are higher than the earth, so are my ways higher than your ways and my thoughts than your thoughts.**

Father is not divided against Himself, it's **our** understanding that is divided against Him because we have not spent enough time in our holy place with Father to get to know Him and how He thinks. In our earthly understanding, we keep trying to get Father to think like we do, but our thinking and our very language itself is flawed. For example, is the following sentence true or false:

Everything in this sentence is false.

You can see my point. If this sentence is true, then it has to be false, but if it is false, how can it be true? For most of us, the logic system built into our culture and our thinking dates back to the Greek philosopher Aristotle. It is a logic system that works most of the time, but also allows things that, well, are not logical. Father's "logic system" is not flawed like ours is, and to learn His logic, we have to learn Him. How do we learn Him?

How Do We Learn Him?

When I used to install sound systems, we defined *noise* as any unwanted signal or sound. Is your life too noisy and filled with things you don't really want? Are you, yourself, too noisy?

Most of us have practiced being noisy all of our lives on multiple levels. We are uncomfortable in the silence of our own minds. We feel compelled to have external music, programming, communication, games and other noise that also mask out the still, small, whisper voice of our Father.

The bigger challenge comes when you turn off and tune out all the external noise, and then you find that you have internal noise. You finally put yourself in a place to be quiet and focus on worshipping in the beauty of holiness, and you are flooded with internal noise. Your mind goes crazy with all the things you need to get done, all the people you need to contact and all the time you are "wasting" here listening for our Father's leading. Then you start feeling hungry, then you get this little itch and you just can't get comfortable, and you find that your body is as noisy as your mind. What does our Father say about quietness?

> **Isaiah 30:15 For thus said the Lord God, the Holy One of Israel, "In returning and rest you shall be saved; in quietness and in trust shall be your strength." But you were unwilling,**

Did you know that it takes 6–12 months for a new habit to become ingrained in your behavior? Your brain will "hard wire" your repetitive behaviors into habits so you don't have to rethink them every time you do them. This is why old habits are hard to break. This is why you can go to work and not remember if you locked your door—locking the door is a habit that does not require you to think. This is why you go home from work and forget to get milk and bread at the store—getting the milk and bread is not your usual habit. These things become ingrained habits and so you just do the habit instead of thinking about it.

If you have practiced being noisy all your life, by now you will have perfected the habit of being noisy. In doing so, have you missed knowing our Father in ways He wants you to know Him? One of the things we know about in life on earth, when we stand before a high official a judge or someone who commands respect, we need to be quiet, to listen and to pay attention. It takes practice to be quiet before Father. To get started we can practice a few minutes of quiet before Him, and extend our quiet as we become more patient in our practice and His presence fills us.

Let me say that I have a friend who speaks of experiencing the presence of our Father in a way that I desire to experience Him too. My friend shared that sometimes he would start to pray and wait on Father, and Father's presence would be so strong that he could no longer speak. Sometimes it is enough just to be together in His presence, for when we are truly in the awe-filled presence of our King of All Creation, is it a surprise that we cannot speak at all? The other amazing thing my friend shared is that sometimes his quiet time would feel like minutes and actually last for hours.

Considerations for Your Playbook:

How can we allow time in our days just to worship and be in Father's presence?

How can you carry a sense of His presence in your work throughout your day?

If there was a time when you were peculiarly aware of Father's presence, whether at church, work or other time and place, what was this like?

Practicing His Presence in Your Heart

I understand that practicing the presence of Christ throughout your day can be inwardly difficult if not outwardly almost impossible. I have already mentioned how we humans tend to focus primarily on one thing at a time and still can carry an attitude of worship throughout the day if we develop the habit.

This is where practice becomes so important. Whenever we practice something, we are moving towards perfection. Just as emergency and rescue teams practice and practice again, and like when we practice a musical instrument, learn a new job or skill or change an old habit, we practice towards improvement. It is like this with our faith too. We have to practice being like Christ. In our practice we stumble, fall backwards, get up and keep going towards perfection in Him. It is a relief to know that we are not expected to be perfect from the start, but that perfection is coming.

> **1Corinthians 13:10 but when the perfect comes, the partial will pass away.**

Think about something you do at work every day. It might be communicating with someone, fixing things, building something, having meetings or any of the things required by your work. Imagine the different ways you would do these things if Christ Jesus physically would be there to help you. What kind of help would Christ be giving you? Practice His presence, for He has said He will never leave or forsake us.

Christ Jesus was a carpenter's son and so am I. From a very young age, I would watch my father work and he would give me little things to do that either would helpful to him or at least keep me occupied and out of the way. As I got older I would help him build cabinets, do a variety of repairs and sometimes work with a crew of builders. My Dad made the work fun and we would kid each other and laugh. We would talk about life, work and family. He taught me how to do a quality job and to expect decent pay, and when we worked with the whole crew, the quality work got done along with expanding the fun to everyone. It made the work easier and inviting to do. When I think of Christ Jesus as a carpenter's son, I imagine him getting the work done with a cheerful attitude and a focus on quality work.

The Christ that I practice being with me in my work is wise, loving and engaging. He understands my pains and insecurities. He has a sense of humor and encourages me at every turn. What is Christ like that you find working with you?

Inwardly we can practice the presence of Christ at any time. What about outwardly? You control certain things in your life and your environment. At work, you have your tools and materials, your procedures and habits, your vehicle or work station, yourself and your surroundings. Often we can add reminders to worship at our work space such as a family picture or a Bible, or if we get a regular break time it can become a short bless and praise time.

Some of us work in highly regulated jobs that specify what is allowable for our clothing, our work space and our behavior. Some of us work in jobs that require a great deal of focus and attention. In these situations, we might have to create reminders by associating things in our work with who we are in Christ. I recall the story of how even a small coin can bring us into a sense of Father's presence, the author is unknown at this time.

> A wealthy employer invited an employee and his wife to dinner. As they were entering a very fine restaurant, the employer stopped to pick up a penny from the ground and look at it for a few seconds. Throughout dinner the wife's thoughts turned to her amazement that the wealthy employer stopped to pick up such a small thing as a penny and hold it as if it were made of gold. When she casually asked if that penny held some unusual value, she was surprised as his response. He asked her to read the words on the penny, and stopped her when she got to the words that said, "In God we trust."
>
> The employer explained, "If I trust in God, the name of God is holy, even on a coin. Whenever I find a coin, I see that inscription. It is written on every single United States coin, but we never seem to notice it!
>
> When God drops a message right in front of me telling me to trust Him. Who am I to pass it by? When I see a coin, I pray. I stop to see if my trust IS in God at that moment. I pick the coin up as a response to God; that I do trust in Him. For a short time, at least, I cherish it as if it were gold. I think it is God's way of starting a conversation with me. Lucky for me, God is patient and pennies are plentiful!"

In this story we see that something as plentiful as a coin can remind us to seize a moment for worship.

Sometimes it can be important to change your environment. For example, I have mentioned Koinonia Farm near Plains, Georgia, USA is the birthplace of Habitat for Humanity. The people work the farm and their missions and they have created an environment of worship and Christian community. If you work on the farm, you start the day with corporate worship in the chapel. They ring a bell three times a day to remind you to take a break for prayer and refreshment.

> **Romans 8:26 Likewise the Spirit helps us in our weakness. For we do not know what to pray for as we ought, but the Spirit himself intercedes for us with groanings too deep for words.**

This is not to say that the environment they have created has eliminated all sense of their human condition. They still have to deal with feelings, relationship issues, and running a business, but they have chosen to hold each other accountable to Christ in an attitude of worship and loving care. They help each other practice the presence of Christ each day.

Considerations for Your Playbook:

Think about being aware of God's presence at work.

Christ Jesus is your daily colleague at work, what kind of personality does he have?

What do you control at your work that you can change in order to practice your faith there (perhaps a coin in your pocket)?

What will change as you become more aware of the Holy Spirit being present and worshipping Father with you?

Who will help you practice the presence of Christ each day?

Your Ability to Bless God

Psalm 103:1 Bless the LORD, O my soul: and all that is within me, bless his holy name.

Genesis 2:7 then the LORD God formed the man of dust from the ground and breathed into his nostrils the breath of life, and the man became a living creature.

Have you ever seriously considered that you, being the pile of dust that you are, have the ability to bless the Living, Loving God, the Creator of the whole universe? Remember God's vision: for us to be His people, and for Him to be our God. Just how do you expect to learn to be God's people, and to truly make God to be your God?

I believe it starts in your heart and your home. In your heart, you want to be, do and have all that Father wants us to be, do and have. This starts with our desire to please Father, but how do we know how to please Father? A couple of ways would include Bible study and making time to be in His presence.

Study the Bible

Micah 6:8 He has told you, O man, what is

good; and what does the LORD require of you but to do justice, and to love kindness, and to walk humbly with your God?

In the Bible, Father tells us what is good and what He requires of us. He tells us how to be perfect before Him.

Hosea 6:6 For I desire steadfast love and not sacrifice, the knowledge of God rather than burnt offerings.

In these verses from Micah and Hosea, I find that our Father wants us to listen to Him, learn about Him, walk with Him; in short, Father wants a close relationship with us. How do you get to know anybody who desires a close relationship with you? You spend time with them.

The other thing is that you don't want to disrespect the other person that you're getting to know. We see in the Bible that even though Saul was scared and wanted to gain the favor of the Lord, he was disobedient. Instead of waiting for the priest to do the offering, he did it himself.

1 Samuel 13: 12 I said, 'Now the Philistines will come down against me at Gilgal, and I have not sought the favor of the Lord.' So I forced myself, and offered the burnt offering." 13 And Samuel said to Saul, "You have done foolishly. You have not kept the command of the Lord your God, with which he commanded you. For then the Lord would have established your kingdom over Israel forever. 14 But now your kingdom shall not continue.

The consequences of disobedience can be costly if you know

what to do and don't do it. It can cost you a relationship with a friend, and it can become an obstacle between you and our Father. The Bible offers guidance on how to please Father and enjoy His presence. It is our guide on learning to know God and what to do or not do in our worship.

Make Time to Be Present in His Presence

When we are getting to know someone, we make time to meet together and share our experiences, thoughts, attitudes and dreams. How do we make time to do this with our God—to be present in His presence?

We make appointments with important people such as doctors, teachers and lawyers. We agree with friends when we will meet for dinner or get together for fun. We usually have a set time when we need to be at work and we make appointments with customers and associates to forward our business together. What about having a God appointment time for you to be present with God? What about a God appointment time at home and at work? Reserve the time for Father and see what He does with this time.

It can be important to find a time that fits. Many of us find that if we make this time early in the morning or late at night, we simply go to sleep instead of enjoying the presence of Father. I find it works best for me in the mornings once the bed is made, I have done some stretching and exercising and am wide awake, but before I go out of the bedroom. After exercising, I am wide awake, but as soon as I step outside the bedroom, I am already engaged in my day. I need to keep that morning niche, between exercise and stepping outside the door, dedicated to blessing the Lord, and dedicated to being present in His Presence.

We know that work can be unpredictable. Some of our work requires us to deal with customers, problems, breakdowns and a variety of inconsistencies and interruptions during the work day. This is why it is important to practice worship at home or in a regular *prayer closet* location. If you have never practiced His presence before, it can take some practicing at home to withstand the distractions of the workplace.

Giving Father Control of Your Thoughts and Your Mind

When you start something new, it can be easy to become distracted or bored with the process. We have had much practice in thinking about the world and the situations around us. We have practiced thinking about our work, our friends, our activities and fun, our human relationships and how we want to do things. We have practiced being worried about our loved ones, our jobs, what is going on is our world and our faith. Yes it is good to think of these things—but at the proper time.

It is not unusual for these practiced thoughts to invade our time with Father. The Apostle Paul made mention of this:

> **2Corinthians 10:5 We destroy arguments and every lofty opinion raised against the knowledge of God, and take every thought captive to obey Christ,**

Practicing His presence and taking control of your thoughts can be quite a spiritual challenge. I began to worship with a small group of people each week who waited expectantly for Father to lead our worship. We waited in silence until someone felt led to sing a hymn or share a message. I spent my first weeks there dealing with every other thought in my head that you might imagine. I would start worshipping Father, and next thing I realize is that I am thinking about a problem at work or something I said. I refocus on Father and then catch myself thinking about something somebody else said or did. I refocus on Father and then start thinking about something I want and need to do, or I doze off, or all of this and more.

This is the reason we call it practice—it takes practice and time to develop your spiritual senses and discernment. It takes practice and time to retrain ourselves away from the troubles of the world to the peace of our Father. Be gentle and patient with yourself.

It takes practice and time to
retrain ourselves away
from the troubles of the
world to the peace of our Father.
Be gentle and patient with yourself.

Waiting for Father

When we are needy or have feelings of urgency or fretfulness, there often is the desire to approach Father without acknowledging who He is. We want to take care of our business at hand and go through our list of needs and wants, and we want to do this as soon as possible in our prayers. True, sometimes things can be so troubling that all you know to pray is, "Lord help me."

We forget that Father knows our needs and our wants even before we pray.

> **Isaiah 65:24 And it shall come to pass, that before they call, I will answer; and while they are yet speaking, I will hear.**

We must remember to acknowledge Him and wait for Him. This is what I mean by purely worshipping Father with a sense of Who He Is, in His greatness and awesomeness.

> I remember as a child, seeing a huge hydroelectric power dam in the evening. In the darkness, the dam was well-lit at its base, I could hear the hum of power in the wires, and looking up into the night sky it seemed as if the dam ex-

tended into the heavens. It was so big, and I was so small. At that time, this dam was the biggest, most powerful thing I had ever experienced. I recall thinking that God must be even bigger and more powerful—more awesome—than this dam.

To worship is to acknowledge Father in His goodness, His faithfulness, His awesomeness. It is to recall the great things He has done and affirm the great things He will do. It is to practice and to seek and to wait for a sense of His presence, and then to bless Father and enjoy His presence. Practice waiting on the Lord.

Bless the Lord, O My Soul!

What does it mean to bless the Lord?

Bless - to extol as holy; glorify, "Bless the name of the Lord."

To bless the Lord our God is to enter into a pure form of worship with Him without expecting anything in return. It is to seek Father's heart out of love and the desire to be in His presence. How do we bless the Lord? Let us look to some of the Psalms of praise. Notice how these Psalms mention Father's goodness towards us, and we bless Him to the depths of who we are.

> Psalm 103:1 Bless the LORD, O my soul: and all that is within me, bless his holy name.
>
> 2 Bless the LORD, O my soul, and forget not all his benefits:
>
> 3 Who forgiveth all thine iniquities; who healeth all thy diseases;
>
> 4 Who redeemeth thy life from destruction; who crowneth thee with lovingkindness and tender mercies;
>
> 5 Who satisfieth thy mouth with good things; so that thy

youth is renewed like the eagle's.

6 The LORD executeth righteousness and judgment for all that are oppressed.

7 He made known his ways unto Moses, his acts unto the children of Israel.

8 The LORD is merciful and gracious, slow to anger, and plenteous in mercy.

9 He will not always chide: neither will he keep his anger for ever.

10 He hath not dealt with us after our sins; nor rewarded us according to our iniquities.

11 For as the heaven is high above the earth, so great is his mercy toward them that fear him.

12 As far as the east is from the west, so far hath he removed our transgressions from us.

13 Like as a father pitieth his children, so the LORD pitieth them that fear him.

14 For he knoweth our frame; he remembereth that we are dust.

15 As for man, his days are as grass: as a flower of the field, so he flourisheth.

16 For the wind passeth over it, and it is gone; and the place thereof shall know it no more.

17 But the mercy of the LORD is from everlasting to everlasting upon them that fear him, and his righteousness unto children's children;

18 To such as keep his covenant, and to those that remember his commandments to do them.

19 The LORD hath prepared his throne in the heavens;

and his kingdom ruleth over all.

20 Bless the LORD, ye his angels, that excel in strength, that do his commandments, hearkening unto the voice of his word.

21 Bless ye the LORD, all ye his hosts; ye ministers of his, that do his pleasure.

22 Bless the LORD, all his works in all places of his dominion: bless the LORD, O my soul.

There are times to praise and worship alone as well as to share our praise and worship in assembly together, as in Psalm 111.

Psalm 111:1 Praise ye the LORD. I will praise the LORD with my whole heart, in the assembly of the upright, and in the congregation.

2 The works of the LORD are great, sought out of all them that have pleasure therein.

3 His work is honourable and glorious: and his righteousness endureth for ever.

4 He hath made his wonderful works to be remembered: the LORD is gracious and full of compassion.

5 He hath given meat unto them that fear him: he will ever be mindful of his covenant.

6 He hath shewed his people the power of his works, that he may give them the heritage of the heathen.

7 The works of his hands are verity and judgment; all his commandments are sure.

8 They stand fast for ever and ever, and are done in truth and uprightness.

9 He sent redemption unto his people: he hath commanded his covenant for ever: holy and reverend is his name.

10 The fear of the LORD is the beginning of wisdom: a good understanding have all they that do his commandments: his praise endureth for ever.

How does each of these Psalms expand more about worshipping Father in praise, blessing and recounting his awesomeness and His care for us?

Psalm 113:1 Praise ye the LORD. Praise, O ye servants of the LORD, praise the name of the LORD.

2 Blessed be the name of the LORD from this time forth and for evermore.

3 From the rising of the sun unto the going down of the same the LORD'S name is to be praised.

4 The LORD is high above all nations, and his glory above the heavens.

5 Who is like unto the LORD our God, who dwelleth on high,

6 Who humbleth himself to behold the things that are in heaven, and in the earth!

7 He raiseth up the poor out of the dust, and lifteth the needy out of the dunghill;

8 That he may set him with princes, even with the princes of his people.

9 He maketh the barren woman to keep house, and to be a joyful mother of children. Praise ye the LORD.

Sometimes it helps to have a Psalm that is short.

Psalm 117:1 O praise the LORD, all ye nations: praise him, all ye people.

2 For his merciful kindness is great toward us: and the truth of the LORD endureth for ever. Praise ye the LORD.

Go ahead and make it personal. How come you would want to bless Father? It does not have to be a dread task to think and acknowledge why you are thankful. As one example, my personal list of thankfulness for right now would fold into my praise time. It might go something like this:

> Father, I come before You now to bless Your name and give thanks for Your goodness, for Your holiness and for being the most awesome Being that I can ever know. Thank You for
>
> > Love that does not keep score
> >
> > Joy that is Your joy and my strength
> >
> > Peace that passes all understanding amidst a fallen world
> >
> > Your care for my family and me
> >
> > You take away my worry and replace it with faith
> >
> > You show me Your way each day in my work
> >
> > You give me another day to share Who You Are with others
>
> Bless You Father, O my soul and all that is within me. Amen.

Considerations for Your Playbook:

As you engage yourself to worship Father, what are some things you can to do carry your worship to work?

When you think about blessing the Lord, how do you feel?

If you practice naming seven **personal** things per day for which you are thankful, starting now, what would they be?

Definition of Worship

Worship is an "adoring reverence or regard."

Father is waiting for us to approach Him in an attitude of worship. In our doing so, He makes His presence known to us. It is easy for us to practice not knowing His presence, all we have to do is get too busy or too focused on other things such as our problems, debts, relationships and worries, games and entertainment, sports and school. Then we miss worshipping Father who made us for His purpose of being worshipped.

Did I mention that it takes practice? How often do we miss His presence because we do not take the time to worship Him in our day, in each hour or moment?

In our culture, we can suffer from a worship-like, addictive focus on business success and the idols of our culture such as money, houses and sex. How can we go to work and worship God instead of business and its idols? How would you set aside some minutes throughout your day to worship by praising, blessing, thanking or simply being quiet before Him with adoring reverence and regard?

Considerations for Your Playbook:

> When do you/will you structure your day so you practice adoring reverence and regard for Father?

What would it be like to have Christ physically present and worshipping Father with you?

I have known people who would set a place at the dinner table for Christ Jesus. What do you think of making space for Christ Jesus by having something connected with your work that reminds you of your faith, your calling, your challenges and your relationship with Father? How do you make Him to be your God and you to be His people?

Working for the Lord

We are urged to be aware of the Lord at all times. When work is new, complicated or hard, it can be difficult to be mindful of the Lord and do the task at the same time. How can you train yourself to carry an attitude of worship and still focus on the job at hand?

Ecclesiastes 9:10 Whatsoever thy hand findeth to do, do it with thy might;

Colossians 3:23 And whatsoever ye do, do it heartily, as to the Lord, and not unto men;

Ephesians 5:19 Speaking to yourselves in psalms and hymns and spiritual songs, singing and making melody in your heart to the Lord;

Colossians 3:16 Let the word of Christ dwell in you richly in all wisdom; teaching and admonishing one another in psalms and hymns and spiritual songs, singing with grace in your hearts to the Lord.

There are a couple of related things I would like to say here. First, I have found it very challenging myself to be mindful of the Lord at all times, especially when doing something new or complicated that requires my focus, or when dealing with something unexpected or emotional. Second, I also find it a good thing that in practicing His presence and worship, that I develop an ongoing sense of Father that allows me to respond more and more in a Godly way even when I am not fully mindful of Him. For example, if I am concentrating on getting something done, and I get interrupted, my first thought might be one of irritation and my second thought might be more merciful and full of grace. With practice, my first thought is more likely to be merciful and full of grace.

I cannot emphasize enough of how important it is to dig the well before you need the water. Dig your well of worship deep into the things of God such that you are hydrated with His living water of peace, grace, mercy and wisdom. Drink deep from your well, and in the dry dust storms of life you will not thirst. This is something we must do in advance, do as a regular part of knowing Father and each day finding His joy that flows beneath all sadness and hardship. Again I say, dig your well before you need the water.

Let me share a true story.

> It used to be that sometimes I would be facing a difficult challenge, and I would awaken in the middle of the night and start fretting about it and sometimes stay awake most of the night. Then one day I was alone and praying the Lord's prayer. I started, "Our Father, who art in heaven," and I stopped and said, "Father, how come I'm here alone and praying the word *our*? Doesn't *our* mean there is more than one praying the prayer?" The answer was almost immediate from Christ Jesus, "Just as I prayed this prayer with my disciples, I pray it together with you every time you pray it." I had to think about this before I could fully receive

it, and I was flooded with a sense of joy. My Lord Christ Jesus is here, praying this prayer with me. This was the first lesson.

I continued to pray until I got to the part that says, "Give us this day our daily bread," and then I felt like I had to stop. "*This day.*" We know that for us as Christians, school is always in session and the Holy Spirit is always teaching. This became one of those teachable moments because I knew this lesson immediately: *We are to pray this prayer every day, asking daily for our needs to be met, for our own forgiveness, and for the heart to forgive others.*

What lessons I did learn! I began to pray this prayer every day at the beginning of my meditation time. When I shared my lessons with my wife, we started praying the Lord's prayer every day before we got out of bed. Then I noticed a miracle happened. When facing those difficult challenges, sometimes I would still awaken in the middle of the night and start to fret, but my response had changed. I had been practicing the praying of the Lord's prayer every day for months, and I would pray this prayer and stop my fretting. I started blessing the Lord in the middle of the night and would go back to sleep or calmly plan if there was anything I could do.

I remember the first time I stopped fretting. It surprised me, and I knew in my knower this was because I had been practicing His presence whenever I prayed, "Our Father," and He was being faithful in responding to my prayer. It was Smith Wigglesworth who said, "You have to live ready, because if you have to get ready, it will be too late." Prepare yourself with worship each day. Dig the well before you need the water.

In working on a job or owning a business for the Lord we have to prepare ourselves in advance. We do not meet the Lord when we arrive each day at the job, He is already with us as we go. When we arrive on the job it is not just my job alone, I work the day with Father and for Father, doing everything as unto the

Lord. Acknowledge His presence throughout the day.

> **Proverbs 3:6 In all thy ways acknowledge him, and he shall direct thy paths.**

What does it mean to work for the Lord? What does it mean in terms of honesty, integrity, doing your best, and honoring the Lord in all you do at work? What does it mean in terms of your relationships at work?

Considerations for Your Playbook:

How do you prepare to be with Father as you start your work day?

How do you worship Father as you go through your day?

What happens to your sense of worship when you are interrupted or have to really focus on your tasks?

Dealing with a Really Bad Day at Work

Sometimes we simply have a bad day at work. Sometimes we have trials and persecutions, sometimes we are just doing our jobs and the piano falls on our heads. How can you worship when you are having a bad day or work is just awful? What did Paul and Silas do?

> **Acts 16:23–24. And when they had laid many stripes upon them, they cast them into prison, charging the jailor to keep them safely: Who, having received such a charge, thrust them into the inner prison, and made their feet fast in the stocks.**

Imagine Paul and Silas starting out on a normal day of spreading the Word and ministering the Gospel. They were doing good things in the marketplace, but their good things were seen as not so good by some other folks.

All of a sudden they were taken prisoner and brought before the rulers and charged with breaking the law; what a bad day.

Then they were publically whipped; what a painfully bad day.

Then they were thrown into prison; their painfully bad day got even worse.

The jailor was told to keep them secure, so he put them in maximum security lock down; what a bad day indeed!

How bad was this going to get?

Imagine the beating and the public spectacle they were made to be. Imagine the public opinion and damage to their reputations. What did they do?

> **Acts 16:25. And at midnight Paul and Silas prayed, and sang praises unto God: and the prisoners heard them.**

After having such a bad day, they prayed and sang praises in the presence of other witnesses. What else could they have done? They could have complained about the injustice of it all. They could have cried in the pain of their wounds. They could have proclaimed their innocence for all to hear. They could have threatened everyone with the judgment of God. They could have just sat there in the dark having a pity party and feeling sorry for themselves.

Do you think that they dug the well before they needed the water? Had they already been practicing His presence so that they were able to pray and sing when hardships came? Yes! They had gotten to know the Father to whom they prayed and sang. They had dug a deep well of worship, and having done so they were able to drink deeply from Father's abundant waters of life, and Father responded for His own glory.

> **Acts 16:26. And suddenly there was a great earthquake, so that the foundations of the prison were shaken: and immediately all the doors were opened, and every one's bands were loosed.**

Their chains were broken and suddenly they were at choice: they could stay or make a run for it. They chose to stay, and in making this free choice, our Father used them mightily again. As a result, the jailer and his whole family received Christ and were baptized, and Father was glorified. In the midst of this very bad day, they prayed and praised, and then Father set them free, and in choosing to remain in the jail they still remained free. Did I mention that they had already been practicing His presence?

The Importance of Fellowship

Paul and Silas were there for each other, to support each other and together reach to touch Father's throne of grace and mercy. We are not Paul and Silas, but sometimes, like Paul and Silas, we need someone else to join us in the journey. At times I have been so troubled that I could not find Father on my own. I have had to go to my friends and ask them for prayer and some care.

> I recently received a call from a friend who could not find the Lord in her trouble. She had made a very bad mistake at work that could get her fired from her job, and she had been up most of the night in worry. We discussed that it took her a while to get over the initial shock of how bad the mistake had been, but then she went to tell her supervisor and he already knew what she had done. He appreciated her honesty in coming to him and she still did not know if she would lose her job.
>
> I was able to remind my friend of God's faithfulness and of other times when she had relied on Him and things worked out for the best. I was able to help her re-balance and focus on how Father had walked with her in the past and was walking with her in the present.

When we are having a bad day at work, we must look to Father, our help in time of need. We worship Him in times of need. We pray and sing praises to the Most High God, and we reach out in fellowship to believers around us who help us focus on Father together. We find freedom in the Father through Christ Jesus His Son, our Brother. We have a relationship where we can find rest, freedom and even joy amidst our bad days.

Considerations for Your Playbook:

What would be your favorite prayer and song of praise, especially for bad days?

Who do you call when you need or want fellowship or prayer?

How will you develop your worship habits now so you are ready in the days of tribulation?

Adapt Your Workplace for Worship

When you consider where you work and what your job requires, you usually have the tools you need to do your job. We adapt our work environment to help us focus on our job at hand. Some adapt our vehicles with tool bins or turn our cars into offices. Some equip our workplace with a desk or table, various communication devices and technology. Some include photographs of family and recognition of awards and achievements. If you agree that your primary job is being His people and God being your God, then how might you adapt your workplace for the Godly job at hand?

Knowing that some workplaces do not allow symbols of worship or personal items in our workspace there are other reminders to use.

- In the USA, our coins include the motto, "In God we trust." Simply keeping a coin handy can become a worship reminder. Remember the story of the business owner and the penny?
- If your company has a mission statement on the wall, it could remind you that you have a higher mission to bless the Lord.
- Every doorway can remind us that Christ stands at the door and knocks, and remind us to bless His name for opening

the doorway to our hearts.

Look around you right now. What do you see and how can it remind you to practice the presence of Father?

Even in an office space with no windows, we get to go outside now and then. All nature sings of our Creator. Rocks, plants, trees, flowers, sky, water the air we breathe (take a deep breath) and more can give us a pause to worship and acknowledge Father.

> **Isaiah 55:12 For you shall go out in joy and be led forth in peace; the mountains and the hills before you shall break forth into singing, and all the trees of the field shall clap their hands.**

> **Psalms 19:1 The heavens declare the glory of God, and the sky above proclaims his handiwork.**

Recall that Jacob, who became Israel, set his own pillar in place as a reminder of his encounter with our Father and the promise given to him. Jacob went so far as to name the big rock he placed.

> **Genesis 35:14 And Jacob set up a pillar in the place where he had spoken with him, a pillar of stone. He poured out a drink offering on it and poured oil on it. 15 So Jacob called the name of the place where God had spoken with him Bethel.**

Our minds are powerful tools for maintaining a Godly attitude as well as getting our work done. In our minds, most any tool or object can be associated with Father and with worship. A coffee cup can remind us of the cup for communion, a trash can is for our sins, and a pen or pencil is for writing our name in the Book of Life. We can make anything and everything in our lives to be a reminder for worship.

For those of us who can bring personal items to work, right there next to your family photo, can you put a Bible or some token of faith as a reminder of worship? Can you set appointments or reminders on your calendar to nudge you about worship during the week? If you have a glass top on your desk, what Bible verse or saying might you slip under the glass?

These are a few ideas to help us practice the presence of Father, to remind us that we can develop a sense of worship throughout our days and offer the love and peace of Christ Jesus to all people. You never can tell when the burdens and ambushes of a day will all fall upon you at one moment, and having something to remind you of His presence with make all the difference between doing something to honor your faith or doing that thing you will regret.

Considerations for Your Playbook:

How can you adapt your work environment so it helps you focus on worship?

What are your personal requirements for worship at work?

What are some ways you can train yourself to worship Father during the day?

Your
Work As Worship
Guidebook

We believers share many things in common. We worship Father individually and together. We seek to be His people and to follow Him as our God. We could make a long list other things that we do together.

We also share a creative Father who has made us each different. Father treats us according to what we need in order to grow into solid believers who will carry His Word and His message of love and holiness to a world that needs His love and holiness. He has given each of us different gifts to use for His purpose.

I write this to say that there are some actions that will work for all of us. There are some that will work only for you as an individual. We need to learn from each other and from the Presence as we worship Father and fellowship together. We need to share our sameness and also respect and support our differences. Let us take inspiration and heart in these words from the Apostle Paul:

> **Philippians 2:12 Therefore, my beloved, as you have always obeyed, so now, not only as in my presence but much more in my absence, work out your own salvation with**

fear and trembling, 13 for it is God who works in you, both to will and to work for his good pleasure.

14 Do all things without grumbling or disputing, 15 that you may be blameless and innocent, children of God without blemish in the midst of a crooked and twisted generation, among whom you shine as lights in the world, 16 holding fast to the word of life, so that in the day of Christ I may be proud that I did not run in vain or labor in vain.

Changes can take a lot of energy and planning. Remember to be forgiving of yourself and take care of yourself.

Psalms 103:14 For he knoweth our frame; he remembereth that we are dust.

Whether you call it a guidebook, playbook or simply a journal, develop your work as worship plan and make changes until it works for you. Seek to be God's people and for God to be your God.

Proverbs 3:6 In all your ways acknowledge him, and he will make straight your paths.

Godspeed,

Coach Mack

The Plan: Your Work As Worship Program

Jeremiah 29:11 For surely I know the plans I have for you, says the Lord, plans for your welfare and not for harm, to give you a future with hope.

Many people work better if they make a plan. As the saying goes, if you're not working your own plan, you're working somebody else's. Old habits can be very hard to change, and new habits can be a challenge to maintain. Here is the opportunity to strategize and make your plan to change old habits and develop your worship habits.

Micah 6:8 He has told you, O man, what is good; and what does the Lord require of you but to do justice, and to love kindness, and to walk humbly with your God?

Three Habits in 30 Days

A new habit takes about 30 days to establish, and it takes 6–18 months to become embedded and second nature to us. What will you do for 30 days as a test for yourself and then see if you want to continue this habit for 6–18 months? What three goals will you choose for establishing your new worship habits? Include some things that would be easy and encouraging to you, and some things that would be more of a challenge.

You might or might not make use of the following space for your goals and choice of accountability. Some of us work better with a written guide, but either way, our intent is to draw near to Father that He will draw near to us.

> **James 4:8 Draw near to God and he will draw near to you.**

Goal for getting to know Father

This might include read, study, pray, meditate upon His Word, discussions, a study partner.

____

____

____

Date to start: ________ Date to evaluate:________

❑ I put these dates on my calendar

Goal for developing your sense of worship

This might include practice His presence, thankfulness, praise and bless His name.

____

____

____

Date to start: ________ Date to evaluate:________

❑ I put these dates on my calendar

Goal for adapting your workplace environment

This might include using an object on your desk or in your vehicle as a reminder to worship, or some action such as sending emails or seeing people.

____

____

____

Date to start: ________ Date to evaluate:________

❑ I put these dates on my calendar

My Accountability

Self Check. I will make an appointment with myself to check on my own progress every

____________________________.

Partners. These people have consented to be my partners to support my new habits:

____

____

Your Standards and Boundaries in Christ

Have you ever been in a situation where you started feeling uncomfortable with someone else? Maybe it was something they said, how they said it, or something they did. Chances are good that you started feeling uncomfortable when someone crossed a personal boundary in your life. You might not be aware of all your boundaries until somebody crosses one of them and then you feel uncomfortable.

Your standards and your boundaries always connect with each other. Your boundaries point towards your standards. Clarifying and articulating your standards help you set better boundaries and know how to respond when your boundaries are crossed.

For example, one of my standards is: I honor and respect other people as part of God's creation.

From this standard, I can set several boundaries and ***practice*** how I will respond when those boundaries are crossed:

> I do not yell at other people. If I lose my temper and yell, I will accept responsibility for my temper, ask for forgiveness, and see what I can do to make things right.
>
> I do not allow others to yell at other people when they are around me. If someone is yelling abusively, I will ask that person to stop and give a warning that I will leave, or advise other action I will take if the disrespect does not stop.

> I do not force my beliefs on others. If someone feels like I am pushing my faith on them, I am glad to change the subject.
>
> I do not allow others to force their beliefs on me. If I am uncomfortable or feel like my beliefs are being disrespected, I will politely ask them to change their approach or change the subject. If they continue to disrespect me, I will warn them that I will leave and do so if necessary.

We want to practice our faith, deepen our relationship with God and develop sensitivity and discernment for His leading. Here are some standards and boundaries for you to consider. Use these as a pattern to develop your own. Warning: It can become easy to think of this as your personal checklist for holiness, or to become rigid and legalistic in your practice. Remember the place of grace, mercy and forgiveness when we fail in our faith and practice.

Standard: I seek to honor God in all I do (Col 3:23 Do everything heartily as unto the Lord)

Because of this Standard, I:	To set some Boundaries, I:
Do my best in my work	Ask others to respect my time at work
Carefully choose my entertainment	Don't attend movies that have content that dishonors my faith
Forgive myself according to the Word	Don't allow guilt or shame to control or limit me
______________ ______________ ______________	______________ ______________ ______________

Standard: I draw close to my Father (James 4:8 Draw near to God, and he will draw near to you.)

Because of this Standard, I:	To set some Boundaries, I:
Bless the Lord in my worship (Psalm 103: 1-5)	Do not allow cursing in God's name to go without warning
Carefully choose my entertainment	Focus on what we have, not what we don't have
Train myself with daily worship reminders	Ask others to respect my morning/evening worship
______ ______ ______	______ ______ ______

Standard: I avoid the works of flesh (Timothy 6:11 Flee these things)

Because of this Standard, I:	To set some Boundaries, I:
Have an accountability partner	Don't miss my accountability meetings
Choose healthy places to go	Don't go where I am tempted—I avoid certain places
Keep company with people of high standards	Set firm limits with people I don't know or trust
______ ______ ______	______ ______ ______

Standard: I practice giving (2 Cor 9:7 God loves cheerful giver)

Because of this Standard, I:	To set some Boundaries, I:
I give at least 10% of my time to Father's work	Don't let others distract me into missing this time
I give at least 10% of my income to Father's work	Don't yield to the temptation to overspend
I give cheerfully	Don't allow myself to be run by my needs
______________ ______________ ______________	______________ ______________ ______________

Standard: I help others in need (Galatians 6:10 Do good to all)

Because of this Standard, I:	To set some Boundaries, I:
Will go the second mile with a sense of joy	Will not overextend myself or my resources
I will set good limits on what I do	Tell others what I can do or will not do to help
I will not be shamed or guilted into more	I will speak up when I feel manipulated
______________ ______________ ______________	______________ ______________ ______________

Write Your Own

Standard: ______________________________

____

Because of this Standard, I:	To set some Boundaries, I:
______ ______ ______ ______	______ ______ ______ ______
______ ______ ______ ______	______ ______ ______ ______
______ ______ ______ ______	______ ______ ______ ______
______ ______ ______ ______	______ ______ ______ ______

CPSIA information can be obtained
at www.ICGtesting.com
Printed in the USA
FSOW01n2335230917
38856FS